MW00808613

Developing superpower skills is not only possible but it is something all humans once knew how to do. Training your child to do this will enhance his or her life in unimaginable ways. This book shows you how to look at the mind as an untapped resource, our greatest asset, and invites you to take a different view of our innate mental powers. What you discover may alter the course of your life and the way you perceive and interact with yourself and your children.

KUDOS for *Children Who Know How to Know*

In *Children Who Know How to Know* Elly Molina explains techniques for developing and using ESP, or "intuitive abilities." The book takes us through how a brain develops and works, and then give activities and exercises for developing the natural innate psychic abilities that everyone is born with. Then it goes on to talk about learning to trust these abilities once you have developed them. Although fairly short, the book is packed full of good information that everyone can use. Whether you want to develop your own psychic abilities, help someone else to do so, or simply learn more about them, this book is an excellent resource. ~ *Taylor Jones, The Review Team of Taylor Jones & Regan Murphy*

Children Who Know How to Know, A resource guide for helping children develop and utilize their powerful intuitive abilities, by Elly Molina is an instruction manual for teaching yourself and your children to develop and use intuition, or psychic powers, which the author believes are dormant in all humans. Whether she is right or wrong, the book is an excellent resource for understanding how the brain works as well as ways to make it work more effectively. Giving us both the science behind her theories, as well as practical exercises and activities to make them easy to apply in your own life, *Children Who Know*

How to Know is an excellent resource guide and a very thought-provoking read. ~ *Regan Murphy, The Review Team of Taylor Jones & Regan Murphy*

ACKNOWLEDGMENTS

With heartfelt gratitude, I thank everyone who has come into my life and touched, inspired, and taught me to see life through different lenses. I thank all the many children, their parents, clients, and friends for enriching my life with their presence.

I thank the late, Dr. Delores Beckham, former Principal of IS 145, and Assistant Principal, Rob Nikc, Queens, New York, for providing the opportunity to teach an enrichment program: *The Power to Create.*

Special appreciation to Dr. Henry Reed, for introducing me to his Intuitive Heart Work and his many hours of mentorship.

I thank the fabulous children of the former Children's School of Excellence, Rainier, Washington, where magic truly happened. Thanks to the parents who entrusted me with their children while we created magic.

Thank you, Anthony, for taking this journey across the country with me and becoming a "psi-kid."

Thank you to my friends, Matt and Ana, for continuously encouraging me to write and John D. for his creativity.

Special thanks to Christian de Quincy for editing the original manuscript, and Faith, at BOB.

Thank you, Black Opal Books, for your support and bringing these pages to the world.

Children Who Know How To Know

A resource guide for helping children
develop and utilize
their powerful intuitive abilities

Elly Molina

A Black Opal Books Publication

CHILDREN WHO KNOW HOW TO KNOW
Copyright © 2017 by Elly Molina
Cover Design by John Dispenza
All cover art copyright © 2017
All Rights Reserved
Print ISBN: 978-1-626946-31-6

First Publication: MARCH 2017

Published by Black Opal Books **http://www.blackopalbooks.com**

*This book is dedicated to the intuitive and psychic you.
It is dedicated to creating a new paradigm for education.
May we practice and teach our children to be present,
mindful, and conscious of thoughts, words, and deeds.*

Children Who Know How To Know

TABLE OF CONTENTS

.

Introduction

"The intuitive mind is a sacred gift
and the rational mind is a faithful servant.
We have created a society that honors
the servant and has forgotten the gift."
~ Albert Einstein

This is a fabulous time in history to be a child. Children in the Western world have the highest literacy and survival rate since the mid-1990s. In 2014, more US citizens enrolled their children in alternative, prestigious, private schools than ever before in the history of US education, and parents use new approaches to disciplining their kids. Mindfulness and yoga practices appear more and more in both public and private education. In 2014, Brown University broke new ground by offering a major in Contemplative Studies, the first in North America. As of this writing, more than twelve major universities offer a BA, MA, or PhD in Contemplative Studies. Contemplative Studies "looks at how we think about the world and how we think about thinking." This curriculum spearheads a new approach to education. More schools than ever before now teach children an "I can do it" attitude.

A century ago, people read approximately fifty books during their lifetime. Today, parents invest more in their children's development and education than at any time during the last one hundred years. Today, we witness expanding consciousness, as ideas, once considered fantasy and science fiction, become real, radically altering the future for our children. At no other time since the birth of the European Enlightenment do so many children have opportunities to learn how to develop their intuitive and psychic abilities. Back in the 1950s and 1960s, only three TV shows addressed the topic of psychic or supernatural powers: *The Twilight Zone, One Step Beyond,* and *Alfred Hitchcock.* In the last decade, by contrast, hundreds of movies feature psychic powers, and countless TV series feature psychics, mentalists, and extraordinary phenomena.

While intuition and psychic abilities gain widespread popularity in mass entertainment, the surge of interest in intuitive and psychic ability means that fewer people regard these "paranormal" abilities as just the stuff of fiction.

Remember Robert A. Heinlein's novel, *Stranger in a Strange Land*? His main character, Valentine Michael Smith, the orphaned son of the first astronauts to explore Mars, learns to have full control over his mind and body. When he finds himself back on Earth, US Government agents attack him and, in self-defense, he sends them into a fourth dimension.

When I read Heinlein's book, I wondered: *What if we could learn to do this and could we teach it to children?* The question prompted me to explore my own psychic abilities.

I believe we all once knew how to use telepathic and telekinetic powers (both as young children and historically in the early days of our species), but we lost these abilities during some sort of "dark age." However, today, as more and more people open up to the possibilities of intuition and paranormal powers, a "new renaissance" of interest in these phenomena spreads in the mainstream. Developing these natural innate abilities signals the emergence of a new consciousness.

In a way, this book documents my personal journey, beginning as a highly intuitive and psychic child. Like so many other well-intentioned parents, mine invalidated my intuitive and psychic abilities. I overcame self-doubt, and embraced my intuitive knowing, only as an adult.

As an ESL (English as a Second Language) teacher, I knew I was onto something when I observed non-English-speaking children telepathically communicating with classmates during English lessons. I developed simple telepathic games to teach English to non-native speakers. Years later, while teaching Language Arts in an inner city public school, I taught positive thinking while working on vocabulary and spelling. I wove intuitive development into the standardized curriculum. My students used their intuitive abilities to access knowledge that already existed within them. Their self-confidence increased. They changed their approach to life and learned to accept responsibility for their actions, all helping to create an environment of achievement and excellence. By 2007, my students had achieved exceptionally high test scores; my first practical hands-on training program for intuition in an educational setting had begun.

Part of the NYC middle-school enrichment program, I named the training "The Power to Create." Each session lasted three months. I met weekly with twenty seventh-graders for two hours. As the program gained popularity in the school, the kids began using new vocabulary and produced results. They practiced creating and achieving clear goals, learning to be mindful of the power of their words and their personal beliefs about themselves and the world.

I also introduced a concept of "seeing without eyes," a basic form of remote viewing. Let's look at what this means: remote viewing (formerly known as "clairvoyance") refers to the ability to perceive distant objects without the use of our eyes. This ability can be learned by anyone, and those who practice it regularly, often experience increased success.

After practicing remote viewing, one surprised and satisfied seventh grader, Alan, exclaimed: "It was crazy! I put the blinders over my eyes. First, I couldn't see nothing (*sic*), then I could see where the objects were on the table. I could 'see' what some of them were, even though I had my blinders on. It was freaky! Then I started to really like it. I felt smart. I felt confident. I felt good!"

As the students' accuracy increased, so did their self-confidence in their abilities to achieve higher school grades and to do better work in their classes. Their results continued to amaze me, and my passion for this work grew stronger with each workshop.

In 2008, I left my teaching position in New York City and ventured forth, looking for a place to teach children how to use more of their minds—without limitations or fear of backlash from the establishment.

About forty-minutes southeast of Olympia, Washington, tucked away in a small, remote town nestled among one-hundred-year-old Douglas firs, I found a wonderfully unique opportunity: a small private school, among the avant-garde of an emerging paradigm that aimed to create conscious, mindful human beings.

Throughout the school-day, the children incorporated variations of mindfulness. They learned to master tasks and learn through focused and directed attention. We worked collaboratively to enhance concentration, innovation, "knowingness," and genius (using more of your mind creatively). Our mindfulness exercises taught children how to adapt, change, and develop their brains to achieve a heightened state of awareness.

It is amazing to witness what happens to children when they learn they are responsible for their own behaviors and responsible for their words and actions. Following the exercises, these children were noticeably kinder, gentler, and more loving toward each other and their environment. As we explored the power of mindfulness together, we also included psychic and intuitive development. Working with these children, ages three to twelve, I began to develop a passion and, later, an ability to teach psi-development.

Five days a week, at approximately nine-thirty a.m., a group of twelve young children sat in a semicircle on a blue carpet in their classroom. After reviewing the days of the week and the weather, they sat "crisscross applesauce," (also known in yoga as Easy Seated Pose or the Sanskrit: Sukhasana) with their tiny fingers in what I called the "Zoot" position (the first three fingers of both hands intertwined) and silently waited for me to begin some extraordinary work.

I gave each child a pair of black eye shades (the kind you get on an overnight flight) to place over their eyes. In their safe and private darkness, they primed their minds for the journey about to unfold. Over the past few months, they had practiced visualization, telepathy, telekinesis, and remote viewing—all part of their "Morning Mindfulness" program at this alternative private school, along with regular breathing exercises and learning the art of being present.

Teaching children to develop their visualization and telepathic abilities is easy and natural. I learned this working with them daily. As you read on, I'm sure you will realize how simple it is, too. Occasionally, I'm asked, "Why get children to practice this work? What practical applications can it have?"

My response: For one thing, it teaches patience, focus, and concentration. It teaches confidence and responsibility. Children gain self-confidence while growing up, knowing they can access more of their mind to make choices and decisions more easily—based on a trained and familiar *knowingness* and trusting the accuracy of their intuitive judgments.

The children I work with learn to use more of their minds and use them more creatively. After a few sessions doing this work, children easily performed remote viewing exercises (astonishing to observers unfamiliar with such things). I have seen children predict events with eerie accuracy, turn on flashlights using only their minds, and perform other kinds of telekinesis (mind moving matter). By no means should the children who attend my classes and workshops be considered unique, extraordinary, or precocious. Like other average children, they excel because of their willingness to explore and play "outside the box." Every child, teen, and adult has these abilities. We are born with them, and it is up to us to either use and develop them, or allow them to remain dormant as untapped possibilities.

I believe when we begin to develop and use our psychic abilities, we are naturally drawn to doing good and creating peace and unity. As we continue to learn and use increasingly sophisticated technologies, we need, more and more, to teach our children to trust their intuition to make decisions for themselves in all aspects of their lives. Likewise, we adults need to trust our own intuition to know when we can trust others with our children in social settings, and, more generally, to know which policymakers and politicians we can trust to have our best interests at heart.

For the most part, our culture marginalizes and even pathologizes intuition and the development of "super powers." The media, both news and entertainment, spreads the myth that psi abilities lead to evil and destruction. Contrary to common themes in science fiction, I believe that, as we develop intuitive awareness, we also grow in desiring unity and peace. Accessing and using psychic and intuitive abilities increases our conscious awareness and opens us up to an alternative future rather than the one we create by default. Psi abilities promote consciousness and bring us closer to peace, love, joy, and abundance.

I recently had the opportunity to speak with sixty middle school children, and asked: "If you could have one superpower which would it be?"

Overwhelmingly, they responded "telepathy" and "psychic ability." I wasn't surprised. It inspired me to write this book. When we, teacher and pupils, combine telepathy or some other psychic ability with mindfulness and responsibility, I find that many classroom problems disappear and new conversations focus on compassion and shared responsibility. When we express compassion, responsibility, and intuitive awareness, we raise our emotional intelligence. Recent research published in *Psychological Science*, indicates that higher levels of emotional intelligence dramatically improve decision making (Yip and Cote, 2013).

To sum up: Developing superpower skills will enhance your child's life in unimaginable ways. For those of you curious enough to begin, I suggest a basic introduction to developing your and your child's intuitive abilities.

This book shows you how to look at the mind as an untapped resource, your greatest asset. I invite you to take a different view on your innate mental powers and to journey with me through the following chapters. What you discover may alter the course of your life and the way you perceive and interact with yourself and your children.

I have divided this book into seven chapters, providing you and your child all you need to know in order to tap into your psychic and intuitive abilities.

The first chapter discusses intuition and different psychic modalities scientists use and acknowledge. Chapter two moves from psi to neuroscience and delves into how the brain grows and develops in a child. Helping you and your child understand the rudiments of neuroscience (how the brain works) can serve as an excellent "window of opportunity" to introduce the wonders of mind and brain to your child.

Chapter three introduces ABE (acronym for Attitude, Belief, Expectancy). Our attitudes, beliefs, and expectancies provide the context in which we see and understand our world.

In the fourth chapter, I discuss simple changes in language that will affect you and your child's success in developing intuition, psi, and applicable in other areas of life. In Chapter five, I introduce special meditation and brainwave exercises to help you access alpha (relaxed/alert) and deep theta (dream-like creative) states. You will learn how to relax and open channels to higher realms. In Chapter 6, by doing the exercises and activities I describe, you finally get to practice and perfect your own "Jedi" psychic powers. And, most important of all, you can use these exercises to teach your children to access and express their own true psychic abilities.

Chapter 7 includes exercises for exploring possibilities beyond intuitive abilities. Designed for people who wish to explore other intriguing mind-over-matter powers—such as telekinesis, bilocation, spoon bending, and even OBEs (out-of-body experiences)—these exercises will take you to new horizons. As fantastic as all this sounds, you will read stories of real people who report just these kinds of experiences.

Note: This book is *not* about special "indigo children" or any other "special" beings living among us. No fifth-dimensional entities, ghosts, or spirits here. Just us ordinary extraordinary folks with untapped ordinary extraordinary powers.

I wrote this book for everyone genuinely interested in learning how to develop psychic and intuitive abilities.

It expresses my deepest desire to provide you with a hands-on way to learn to trust your own intuition and to give you the tools to teach your children how to access, develop, and trust their own powerful intuition.

Our Higher Self truly knows what is best for us. And so we do well when we listen to and trust this Source. You have everything within you to live a powerful, empowering, and successful life—and to teach these skills to your children.

Chapter 1

What Is Intuition?

"Sailors have an extra sense
that tells them when they are in danger."
~ Richard Connell, *The Most Dangerous Game*

How do we know when someone is following us or staring at us from across the room? Ever wonder how detectives have that uncanny ability to answer correctly "who done it," and how hospice nurses know the exact moment to tell family members not to leave the room when someone in a coma is about to pass over to the other side. Ask a successful stockbroker how he knew to make a trade and you'll hear: "I went with my gut."

People in many professions tap into their "gut feelings" and use their sixth sense just as readily as their other five physiological senses. Trusting in one's consciousness and intuitive capacities turns out to be a significant factor in success.

Albert Einstein famously said:

"A human being is a part of the whole called by us 'universe,' a part limited in time and space. He experiences himself, his thoughts and feelings, as something separated from the rest—a kind of optical delusion of his consciousness. This delusion is a kind of prison for us, restricting us to our personal desires and to affection for a few persons nearest to us. Our task must be to free ourselves from this prison by widening our circle of compassion to embrace all living creatures and the whole of nature in its beauty."

Recent developments in science support Einstein's quote. The scientific principles that form the foundation of our thinking are antiquated and deeply ingrained in our language, thoughts, and perceptions of ourselves and our world. New discoveries in science show we are not separate from our bodies, from our consciousness, or from other people or things. Nature does not contain any empty spaces, or, as Enlightenment philosophers declared: "Nature abhors a vacuum." Just because we cannot perceive the webs of interdependence that connect us all, doesn't mean they don't exist. It is time society as a whole, not just scientists, acknowledged the deep interconnectedness between everyone and the world we live in.

What if we could begin to see ourselves as more than just the center of our own personal universe? What if we could really comprehend that everyone stands at the center of his or her own universe, and that everyone matters as much as anyone else? What if we could intentionally alter our own consciousness to perceive beyond our five senses? What if we agreed that time and space limit us, and that, as Einstein said, we live in an "optical delusion of our consciousness"? And finally: What if we expanded our limited ways of looking at life and the world to include intuition as a fully acknowledged sixth sense?

I believe nature speaks to us and through us as *intuition.* As one of the most powerful forces, intuition holds together unseen aspects of the world, and unites all things—both here on this planet and, indeed, throughout all multiple universes. Intuition serves as the "glue" that unites our internal and external worlds, and communicates between our deepest inner self and the larger "Self" of the universe. Famed psychologist Carl Jung described intuition as a way for us to move beyond the "tip of the iceberg" by "accessing the invisible roots of our conscious thoughts," our collective consciousness and collective unconscious.

A First-Hand Look at Intuition

The word *intuition'* first appeared in English in the 1500s. It worked its way into Middle English from late Latin. *Merriam Webster* defines intuition as "a natural ability or power that makes it possible to know something without any proof or evidence: a feeling that guides a person to act a certain way without fully understanding why: something that is known or understood without proof or evidence."

Carl Jung wrote:

"Then there are certain events of which we have not consciously taken note; they have remained, so to speak, below the threshold of consciousness. They have happened, but they have been absorbed subliminally without our conscious knowledge. We can become aware of such happenings only in a moment of intuition or by a process of profound thought that leads to a later realization that they must have happened; and though we may have originally ignored their emotional and vital importance, it later wells up from the unconscious as a sort of afterthought."

In other words, accessing intuition means accessing the unconscious or subconscious mind, which ultimately includes the collective consciousness of our entire species.

Some neuroscientists claim intuition might actually be located in the limbic system of our brains, often referred to as the "emotional brain" found buried within the cerebrum, which also includes the outer layer or neocortex, often called the "thinking brain." We will cover more of this in Chapter 2.

Despite all the advances in neuroscience and technology, for most people today, the word "intuition" still conjures up the mysterious realm of the unknown. We talk about "trusting it," "believing in it," "not believing in it," and so on. Nevertheless, throughout the ages, all cultures have universally recognized this "internal knowingness" that lies beyond language and can be accessed only through feeling or embodied sensation. Instinct dominates the behaviors of all the lower kingdoms of nature. However, since higher, more evolved animals—such as dolphins, apes, and humans—exist in an unbroken ancestral biological line all the way back to the lower animals, it should be no surprise that instinct also dictates much of our everyday behaviors, too. However, in addition to instinct (limbic system) we humans also have the ability to use reason (cerebrum and neocortex).

In Western culture, we often refer to intuition as a "gut feeling." People frequently talk about "having hits," "following a hunch," or "a feeling I can't explain." Even though intuition doesn't have any location in the brain or body (because it's a non-physical event in consciousness), people sometimes describe it as intimately associated with particular areas of the body. For example, they might describe it as a "visceral feeling," like having it hit you in your gut; other times, chills may overcome you, or your pulse may quicken. No matter which form it takes, even as subtle as a small voice saying "do this today," that's intuition guiding you. This mysterious knowingness connects us all to a universal consciousness.

Let's look at the term "gut feeling." This sensation actually resides in your abdomen. "Gut feelings" happen so rapidly we need to pay close attention and learn to interpret the messages quickly. The "gut instinct" runs through our central nervous system and produces a quick physical reaction. Again, various names exist for this process; however, if we honor it, in every case a rapid embodied sensation either compels or repels us toward or away from something.

When compelled toward something, we usually feel good about it—excited, light, positive, happy. Also, our bodies often move in a slight, forward motion toward what compels us. By contrast, when repelled, we instinctively tend to move away from whatever repels us. We feel unsure or uncomfortable. We sense something "off" or "wrong." However, in modern culture, our rational minds often second-guess our gut feelings, and then invalidate our instincts with logical thoughts and justifications. Each of us can relate to such experiences: times when we did not listen to our "gut," and ended up regretting that. However, times when we heeded our gut instincts, we felt empowered. Our intuition enables us to understand things instinctively, without conscious reasoning. I will be using the words "intuition" and "instincts" more or less synonymously, so you can begin to practice trusting your "gut" while you learn to develop trusting your intuition.

The following examples will help you identify times in your own life when you trusted your "gut instinct" and your intuition:

As a parent, you may remember these (or similar) experiences:

1. looking for a caretaker for your child.
2. evaluating daycare centers, pre-K, or other educational facilities for your child.

While, of course, checking credentials and recommendations matters, you also need to learn to trust your own intuition, and rely less on "objective" justifications.

Everyone has instinctive and intuitive ability. It is not some rare gift bestowed upon a select few. Rather, it is as much a part of us as the ability to speak, read, run, and eat.

Children, in particular, possess strong intuition. Unfortunately, far too many well-meaning parents suppress or invalidate their children's intuitive abilities—for example, saying "that's not so," or "everything is okay," when in reality everything is not okay, and the children *know* that. This kind of invalidation by parents shows up later in life when children grow into adulthood and no longer trust their intuition or natural instincts. As a child, people probably told you that what you were feeling and thinking was wrong. When children witness their parents fighting, their mothers crying, and adults say "everything is okay," it invalidates the child's perception, and violates the child's sense of being. I advocate acknowledging the child's concerns and then helping her or him feel safe, while also acknowledging the child's powerful intuitive abilities. When we do the latter, the child experiences validation and trusts his or her own intuition.

Reason helps us to arrive at logical conclusions, step by step, and builds up knowledge. Intuition, however, works holistically by seeing the whole picture in one flash of insight. Reason leads to *knowledge,* whereas intuition leads to *truth*.

Even though everyone possesses intuition, most of us find it very difficult to put it into words. Because of that, we tend to distrust intuition. We use language to describe reality. We discover something in the world and then use words to express or describe what we've experienced. It's the same way with intuition. You "get a hit" and then need to find the words to match the experience in your reality.

In my work, I have discovered that most of my clients have within them the answers they seek—even when they profess they don't. Clients come to me because they do not trust what they already know from their own intuitive wisdom; sometimes they just aren't ready to acknowledge their own wisdom and inner-knowing. They want confirmation and validation that they were on the "right track."

Intuition means listening to the information we receive from our Self. The term "Higher Self" refers to receiving information channeled to us from a higher Source. If we believe we are all connected, as Einstein said, then we are part of a universal consciousness.

Even though psychic abilities can be difficult to express in words, some basic definitions and vocabulary can help:

1. *Clairvoyance*: The ability to see pictures and symbols in your mind's eye. Sometimes it's only a quick thought.

2. *Clairsentience*: Also known as "gut feeling," this can come as a general feeling of anxiety or being ill-at-ease. Often, we don't understand why we have the feeling until the event has transpired and the feeling leaves.

3. *Clairaudience:* This refers to hearing voices and sounds without any input from our ears or other senses.

4. *Claircognizance*: The ability to just know without cause.

5. *Clairgustance*: refers to the ability to taste-at-a-distance without the use of our tongue or taste-buds (think of Matthew McConaughey in *True Detective* when he tastes metal at a crime scene).

You have probably had some, or all, of these experiences, and dismissed them as merely your imagination. I wrote this book to help people begin to move away from self-doubt and cynicism about these "anomalous" abilities. Although psi phenomena still meet with much skepticism and doubt, I believe we need to teach our children to use and cultivate the natural intuitive sense that exists within each of us.

Reader Notes

Chapter 2

How Children's Brains Develop and Work

Within the past few years, neuroscience has given us remarkable insight into how the human brain develops. Research shows that within a week of conception the brain begins to develop, already with about 100 billion neurons. These brain cells travel to genetically specified destinations while connecting with one another in the most extraordinary way. Even during the prenatal period, busy brain cells already send and receive messages. By the time the child is born, billions of nerve cells form an amazingly intricate web of connections.

Some of the most important neural connections develop during the first few months of life. During this crucial developmental stage an immense amount of brain activity takes place. The brain continues to grow and develop and, simultaneously, important interactions occur between infant and mother (and other humans), and with its surroundings. These early interactions lay a foundation for the developing sense of self.

We know that genetics do not solely determine brain development. Using sophisticated brain imaging techniques, scientists study rates of development from infancy to young children. For example, babies create approximately 250,000 neurons per minute in their early years following birth and then spend the next few years wiring them together. Given such rapid rates of growth, it's no surprise, as research reveals, that the brains of infants and very young children exhibit high activity and receptivity. In fact, exposure to just a few hours of information during infancy can have more impact on brain development than months of learning during an adult's life. We now know that neurons are not linked at birth, and that new synapses (junction points) form as new "wiring" (axons and dendrites) develop.

These synaptic links connect various parts of the developing brain, and they grow as a result of interactions between the child and his or her world. As synapses multiply, the messages passing through the brain increase as well.

These neural connections influence the child's ability to learn, and connections form through direct stimulation from the environment.

Infants do not see the world the way an adult does. Because they have very different (underdeveloped) perceptual equipment, they naturally take their perceptual cues from adults and their environment. As a result, children learn to perceive and experience reality "through the eyes" of their caregivers. As they observe what goes on around them, the infants' brains filter, organize, and interpret sensory input according to what their brains have learned—that is, according to how their day-to-day experiences shaped the wiring of their neurons and synapses.

As the child's brain continually develops at different times and rates new "windows of opportunity" open up for a limited span of time. During these "windows," the brain remains especially receptive, and new neural connections develop with ease and fluidity. In this book, I will focus more on the brain's wave states, than on the child's cognitive and emotional development.

The human brain produces four major brainwave states—called *beta* (high activity), *alpha* (relaxed/alert), *theta* (drowsy/sleepy), and *delta* (sleeping/trance). The specific frequencies of each wave can be measured using an electroencephalogram (EEG), an electronic monitoring device that detects electrical activity in the brain. EEG images of beta brainwaves show electrical impulses close together, whereas alpha waves spread out; theta and delta, spread out even more.

Exactly what happens in the brain during the first few months of an infant's life remains uncertain; however, we do know infants' brains display a lot of delta, the deep, very slow wave state. Adults display delta usually when asleep, unconscious, or catatonic, with very little activity in the neocortex the center of higher mental functions for humans and other mammals. Because the infant's brain waves run at such a deep level, their brains rapidly absorb information unconsciously. In this state, the brain processes and records a great amount of information about the environment, language, caregivers, and self—all at deep unconscious levels, stored for future reference.

The research data do not conclusively indicate how long infants remain in deep delta, although some researchers have recorded this delta states lasting for up to two years. The neocortex (the thinking brain) operates at exceptionally low levels during this time.

Sometime between two and six years, children's brain waves move into the theta state, faster than delta. In adults, theta indicates REM (dream) sleep, a brainwave frequency also associated with learning and memory.

During theta, children remain highly impressionable. Like sponges, they absorb everything around them from their parents, caregivers, teachers, books, TV shows, and first-hand experiences. Filters for judgement or discernment, have not yet developed, so this information gets stored and embedded in the subconscious mind. Theta connects us to the world of imagination, creation, fantasy, even a certain kind of "knowingness" and "oneness," and children have this in abundance with little or no critical, rational thinking or judgement. They tend to believe whatever adults tell them. The information goes straight into their unconscious. Because of this, parents need to be aware of the kinds of information their children pick up.

In *Trusting What You're Told: How Children Learn from Others* (Belknap Press, 2012), Paul L. Harris discusses how we are biologically destined to learn from one another: "A dominant metaphor for young children's cognitive development is that the child is a scientist who does hands-on experiments, such as with things that float or sink, and revises his or her ideas about the world like a scientist." Harris goes on to say: "By contrast, anthropologists don't do experiments, certainly not on the culture they are studying; rather they master the language, observe carefully, and engage in long conversations with trusted informants, especially when they are puzzled. Children, like anthropologists, are trying to make sense of the culture they live in, including its beliefs and values."

Harris states that children's willingness to listen to and trust other people makes them susceptible to all kinds of things. "They are creatures of their culture." Harris says. "They'll swallow, for better or for worse, the assumptions of the culture." Based on my own personal experience with children and on data from brain research on young children, I agree with Professor Harris.

With new information from neuroscience, especially on brain development, we know more about neuronal plasticity than ever before. For example, we know that cells that "fire together, wire together," and that habits, beliefs, attitudes, and expectancies form as early as three years.

In 1937, Napoleon Hill published, *Think and Grow Rich*, where he stated: "What the mind of man can conceive and believe, it can achieve." Hill used empirical evidence to make that claim, and now data from neuroscience support this statement. Back in the early 2000s, the Children's School of Excellence in Washington State created a program based on quantum physics and neuroscience titled "Mind Leap," designed to teach children to "jump within." The children, who ranged from three to fourteen, learned brain physiology, concentration, lateral thinking, and natural awareness. Each morning, the school day would start off with exercises in one of these areas. The children learned to experience quiet states of mind and to go within, quieting their minds, allowing their internal chatter to cease.

By directing their focus to a battery-operated flickering candle, the younger children sat perfectly still, cultivating focus and quieting their minds. During these ten minutes, they learned to focus on the candle and to practice returning their attention to the candle whenever their mind wandered. This practice taught them to sit quietly and silently, focus on being present, quiet the mind and learn not to allow discomforts of the body to distract them. Research now confirms that the ability to maintain self- control forms a key ingredient for higher emotional intelligence (Yip and Cote, 2013, Yale University). Children between three and six have an easy time doing this because their brains naturally operate in the slower theta frequency. Theta waves show a right-brain hemisphere dominance, which also plays a vital role in successful intuitive development—presenting a perfect window of opportunity for introducing psychic and intuitive work at this point with children and teaching children to control their bodies, whereby developing their emotional intelligence for the future.

Given these findings, we can see the value of introducing children to the possibilities and potentials of psychic abilities at an early age. My own research and work with children between the ages of four and six, clearly demonstrate their readiness, willingness, and ability to perform telekinesis and remote viewing with uncanny accuracy. Without filters, and proving to themselves they could do it, children can strengthen the neural connections associated with a belief that psychic abilities are easily doable and real.

We all have this ability; however, by the time we enter our teens, society teaches us that ESP and PK cannot be real, and we "install" filters that block us from exercising these abilities. We do, of course, still have them, it's just that we come to believe we don't, and have neural connections in our brains that reinforce this belief—and so we stop trying. Lack of use leads to atrophy of our natural psi abilities. In one important sense, we all need to become again "as little children."

If you want your child to trust her or his intuition and develop psychic abilities, then begin opening their minds to these possibilities around three or four years of age. Doing so establishes a belief system that supports the probability of psychic and intuitive phenomena as real and part of everyday experiences.

Once hardwired into the child's brain, a strong belief in the reality of psi makes performing it not only possible, but probable.

Sometime between ages five to eight, the brainwave activity of children moves into the higher alpha frequency where imagination rules, and differences between inner and outer reality begin to dissolve.

Children now start to incorporate deductive reasoning, drawing conclusions about the rules of life. They begin to filter information and try to make sense of whether it works for them. Besides imagination, alpha also accompanies accelerated learning. As an adult, entering an alpha state greatly enhances relaxation and creative visualization.

Once the child reaches twelve and older, the brain's activity increases to a higher frequency, *beta*. Beta brainwaves indicate conscious, analytical, and critical thinking. And whereas alpha, theta, and delta tend to be associated with the right hemisphere, beta shows up mostly in the left brain hemisphere—where logic, objective consciousness, assimilation of information, and perception of "truth" prevail.

Beta waves occur in three ranges. As children grow, they move from low-beta, to mid-beta, and then to high-range beta, where adults mostly function. In beta, we process sensory data and create meaning between our outer and inner worlds. During this stage, cynicism, criticism, and disbelief tend to become more prominent; and so, at this age, introducing psychic and intuitive work needs concrete, "prove-it-to-me" techniques, rather than the kind of "take-it-on-faith" approach that works with younger children.

To sum up: The best time to introduce conversations about psychic ability, intuition, mindfulness, and intuitive heart occurs between ages three to six. In subsequent chapters, I will discuss age-appropriate activities to help introduce conversations about psi and help to establish belief, acceptance, and expectancy.

Reader Notes

Chapter 3

Getting to Know ABE
(Attitude, Belief and Expectancy)

"Your beliefs become your thoughts,
Your thoughts become your words,
Your words become your actions,
Your actions become your habits,
Your habits become your values,
Your values become your destiny."
~ Mahatma Gandhi

It's time to meet ABE, my acronym for *attitude, belief,* and *expectancy.* Let's personify Abe and acknowledge that his power comes from deceiving us into believing he is real and controls our minds—for good or bad. We all have our own friend and foe named Abe. He plays the role of little angel sitting on our shoulder encouraging us, or little devil filling our minds with fear and doubt. Our attitudes reflect our emotions, beliefs, and behaviors toward a particular object, person, thing, or event, and are often the result of experience or upbringing. Our beliefs come from our knowledge, either procedural or declarative.

We gain procedural knowledge by *doing*. We learn to swim by swimming. We learn to cycle by riding a bicycle. Similarly, declarative knowledge comes from *declaring*—expressing or publishing theories assert for the world to hear or read. Almost always, our declarations express what we believe (for example, *The Declaration of Independence* states: "We hold these truths to be self-evident..."). We can debate, question, and argue these theories. Like the declarations that express them, our beliefs also come from our culture, often in the form of inherited conversations passed on from generation to generation. Children accept the assumptions and beliefs of the adults around them and from the larger culture. As soon as children develop to understand and use language, they begin to absorb beliefs from the authority figures around them. Early on, they learn to believe what they are told. Take the example of Santa Claus in Western culture. Research shows that Christian children up to age seven may still believe in Santa. Children in Muslim countries, however, don't share that belief.

If you live in the United States, you've probably heard that Christopher Columbus believed the Earth was round while his contemporaries believed it was flat. If you ask the average North American schoolchild about Columbus, chances are you'll hear the same story today. However, that version is a myth, since scholars during Columbus's time believed the ancient Greek idea of a spherically shaped Earth.

In *Understanding Beliefs* (MIT Press, 2014), Nils J. Nilsson conducted extensive research into where our beliefs come from and how they constitute a large part of "knowledge" about the world. He refers to some cultural beliefs as "the belief trap"; we often hold onto beliefs even when they don't stand up to critical evaluation. We can avoid the belief trap by sharing our beliefs with others and allowing them to challenge us or express their own counter opinions.

The placebo effect stands as a striking example of how beliefs can affect our bodies. The effect occurs when people report improvements in, or disappearance of, symptoms after taking medications containing no ingredients that could cause a symptom relief (usually the "fake medicine" is just sugar pills).

Here, a reputable source or trusted authority (e.g., physician or therapist) tells the patient that the "medication" will improve the condition. Despite lacking any efficacious medicine, the sugar pill "seems" to bring about healing. Of course, the sugar pill doesn't work "magic"; somehow, the patient's *belief* that he or she has taken effective medicine produces the result. *Somehow* the placebo pill *works*. (Medical science still does not understand how beliefs in the mind can affect what goes on in the body.)

Nevertheless, brain imaging studies show the power of the placebo effect: when patients simply *believe* they have taken real medication, the same areas of the brain light up as if they had, indeed, taken the real thing. In a word: *our beliefs can significantly impact our bodies.*

Throughout history, and even today, people willingly die for their beliefs. Some of us argue for our beliefs to the point that we change the chemical composition of our bodies. If you have ever argued with a non-believer over one of your "cherished beliefs," think about what happened to your body. Your blood pressure increased, you began to sweat, you experienced rapid heartbeat, and on occasion, you may have lost your temper. Some people even become violent.

Philosopher Arthur Schopenhauer said: "Every man takes the limits of his own field of vision for the limits of the world."

In his mid-nineteenth century *Studies in Pessimism*, Schopenhauer said that man sees the world through his own limited field of vision. We base our personal truths on our belief systems. Beliefs can either limit us or help us create and live fulfilling lives. Imagine if you had only two weeks to live. Would you make different choices right now? What if you learned you won a million dollars in the lottery? How might that alter your beliefs about yourself, about wealth and wealthy people, about your future? Your beliefs determine your desires, fears, expectations, and actions. Your beliefs determine the type of life you have. They determine what you accept or reject as true.

Our experience of the world depends partially on a lower part of the brain called the "reticular activating system" (RAS). It brings relevant information to the forefront of awareness for us to attend to. Think about all the cars you see on the highway as you drive. As soon as I ask you to focus on yellow cars, your brain automatically seeks those out and, as a result, you notice far more yellow cars passing by. That's how it works. It's the same with our beliefs. We focus attention on what we happen to believe to be true, and we filter information to substantiate our beliefs.

A few years ago, I worked with four nine-year-old children. Both children and their parents believed telekinesis (mind moving matter), telepathy (mind-to-mind communication), and remote viewing (seeing distant objects beyond the line of sight) were not only possible, but probable. We experimented with these psi phenomena and the children expected results.

In all my years doing this work, I've seen only two children perform telekinesis and both times they used a domino.

In this experiment, the children lined up a few dominos, then sat perfectly still, hands and body away from their desks. They focused intensely on their dominos and after about twenty minutes, I saw one child's domino vibrate, then fall.

Expectation and imagination form a close connection. When you imagine something clearly, with emotion, it feels real. In one of my workshops, designed for children, ages seven to twelve, and their parents, I asked if they had ever had the experience of thinking about someone who then showed up or called? Everyone raised a hand.

I then asked if they'd ever experienced *deja vu*—the feeling of already having experienced the present situation. The adults and the twelve-year-olds, raised their hands. I shared a few anecdotes about children I had worked with and their experiences with remote viewing. Then I shared my story of *Annabelle and the Domino,* an illustrated children's book inspired by true events. I intended to remove skepticism and doubt. I promised results.

By the end of the workshop, each participant correctly "saw" and described at least one remote object (out of sight). I conduct these workshops with children, teens, and adults, and the results always remain the same: whether because of beginner's luck or psi-abilities, everyone gets a "hit." If you want consistent results, you'll need to take action, and practice, practice, practice— consistently and methodically. Do this, and you will teach your child the power of setting goals, focusing, and achieving.

When we develop our psi abilities, we increase our self-esteem. Our attitudes shift from learned helplessness to taking control and achieving our goals.

It takes a positive *attitude*, genuine *belief*, and clear *expectancy* (ABE) to develop your own and your child's psi-abilities to their fullest potential.

Reader Notes

Chapter 4

Thought and Language
(What We Say "Matters")

"All of nature begins to whisper its secrets to us
through sounds. Sounds that were previously
incomprehensible to our soul now become
the meaningful language of nature"
~ Rudolf Steiner

Thought, energy, and language connect together in intricate ways. Sounds and language express thoughts. The thoughts we think and the words we use can impact our world. Our words carry vibrational frequency, as well as creative force. Our thoughts and words co-create our reality. "Everything is created twice," first through thought, and then in physical reality. Everything you have ever held, used, or seen was first a thought before finding its way into the physical realm. Therefore, all expressed language, whether through self-talk or conversation with others, co-creates your destiny. Language used intentionally and mindfully enhances our ability to access and develop our intuitive and psychic awareness. Russian psychologist Lev Vygotsky believed speech and thought were separate in the early stages of human development.

Today, researchers agree that very young children go through a period of pre linguistic thought. A child will have thoughts but no words to express them. The connection to thought and language develops through the cognitive stages of a child's development. As a child develops, he or she constructs meaningful words. A sound without meaning does not qualify as a word, yet each sound carries a vibration ranging from high to low. The lower the frequency, the "heavier" the energy it carries. The lighter the frequency, the lighter the energy. Sanskrit, a precise and unambiguous language more than 3,500 years old, has been called "the language of sound." The word "Sanskrit" means "language brought to formal perfection." When scientists at NASA worked on creating a precise artificial language suitable for their computers, they found Sanskrit to be the only completely unambiguous human language. Scientists learned that Sanskrit words carry remarkable power in the energy/vibrational field.

Nigel Stanford, a modern-day musician, works with "cymatics" (the science of visualizing audio frequencies) and makes sound visible. It's fascinating to watch and you'll never doubt the power of sound frequencies again. Words are sounds and all sounds have an inherent power through their frequency. Word frequencies vibrate from low to high. Lower frequency sounds and words vibrate in the emotional realm of fear, regret, blame, guilt, hopelessness, grief, and despair. When a person expresses and feels such emotions, it's reflected in their language. Phrases such as: "I wish I had" or "If only I hadn't" carry the emotion and frequency of shame and regret, vibrating at lower frequencies of the energy spectrum. Continued and prolonged use of these phrases habitualizes the experiences and generates more experiences that also vibrationally match those words and feelings. With time, this can cause bodily illness, as well as disturbing the mind. Notice your own body whenever you articulate these, or similar, phrases. See what happens to your physiology.

Moving up the emotional frequency scale we find anger, resentment, anxiety, pain, hate, hostility, and boredom. Expressed verbally, these emotions attract more of the same. And so we encounter "Murphy's Law."

By contrast, higher-frequency emotions and words— such as, happy, cheerful, thankful, grateful, merry, effer-

vescent, love, peace, and joy—produce a subtle, but no-
ticeable and immediate shift in your energy. Try it for
yourself: Speak or read those words and notice the differ-
ence in how your feel. As you begin to incorporate more
of these words in your conversations you will vibrate at a
higher emotional frequency and your experiences will
match these levels. Some people call it "the law of frequency and vibration."

Here's an exercise you can do right now that will
help you notice how conversations affect you. Think back
to some of the conversations you've had today. Notice if
any of these things happened to you and when:

1. You got tired or even exhausted after spending
time with someone.

2. You felt or sensed an immediate dislike for someone.

3. You felt excited and energized in someone's presence.

Reflect on your conversations. Reflect on your word
choices. Do you notice a strong correlation between
these? Start to notice the connections between word
choices and emotions. The more you do this exercise, the
more skilled you'll become at identifying and joining in
conversations that empower you and others to take action.

Empowering conversations raise your emotional frequency. You'll feel better. You'll even look better. Your posture and physiology change. With practice, you can consciously direct and redirect conversations so that everyone feels better just by choosing to use higher frequency words.

Language awareness enhances our ability to develop intuitive and psychic abilities. We learn that what we speak truly "matters" in the literal sense of the word; we understand how each word carries and expresses a creative force. That's why we need to use language responsibly—by paying attention to our communications and to the importance words have in our lives.

Remember the old saying, "Sticks and stones can break my bones, but words will never hurt me?" Interviews conducted with emotionally and physically abused children tell a different story. Words impact us. They carry enough power to influence us throughout a lifetime. Powerful orators, politicians and advertisers know and make use of this. It's important, then, to pay attention to the power of words—our own and others'.

Parents, in particular, need to heed the profound power of words. Responsible parenting and emotional maturity require control over one's thoughts, impulses, and language. Parents need to role-model language as well as behavior.

In my work with parents and their children, I've created a list of words to use and words to lose. Here are a few of the words to lose:

Can't (or *cannot*): Limits possibility. It shuts down the thinking process and leaves no room for creativity.

Should: Teaches children to give up their self-agency, their own power to decide for themselves. "Should" means obligation, duty, or correctness, and typically comes up when criticizing someone's actions, leading to a chronic sense of "not good enough." When we criticize *ourselves* (having internalized our critics' judgments), we set the stage for a lifetime of "I'm not good enough."

I recommend removing all curse and swear words when speaking with children. Other words to lose are "hateful" and "hurtful" words. Whenever possible, refrain from using these words in your personal life.

For an in-depth and fascinating study on the power of words, see Japanese researcher Dr. Masaru Emoto's book *The Hidden Messages in Water*. Empowering words include:

Gratitude: Guides and directs children in the experience of being appreciative, and thankful.

Joy: Allows children to appreciate feelings of happiness and effervescence; familiar feelings from infancy.

Love: The strongest binding emotion and frequency in our universe.

When we impress upon our children the power of spoken words, they experience a shift in how their world and classroom occur for them.

Another powerful communication tool for children: Teach them to take responsibility for their thoughts and actions. I encourage children and their parents to refrain from victim language and victim behavior. We see victim language and victim thought patterns in phrases such as, "He did it to me." "Look what s/he did to me!" These linguistic constructions establish a habitual victim mentality.

Let's look at the following scenario, omitting emotional interpretations, and simply view the events as causes and effects.

Jack and John play together. Jane stands nearby. John pushes Jack and Jack falls into Jane. Jane loses her balance. Jane falls on the ground into a pool of mud from last night's rain. Jane's dress gets splattered with mud.

This describes an actual event in a second-grade elementary class, and prompted the following reaction:

Jane: "Look what Jack did to me!" (I can see the mud on Jane's dress). But Jane's language reveals she perceives herself as a victim. What if the teacher or parent asked simply: "What happened?" An accurate description, without emotional overlays, would go something like: "Jack fell into Jane. Jane fell. Jack did not dirty Jane's clothes. Landing in the mud caused the dirty clothes."

As time consuming as it might be, by isolating these incidences, we can steer children away from victim interpretations and behavior. This small shift creates huge changes in personal responsibility and self-empowerment.

Language influences and shapes the meaning of our experiences, both positive and negative. The more we repeat a thought or phrase, the more we reinforce a memory circuit until it becomes a belief. We then project our beliefs onto what happens outside ourselves. However, much of what we take to be real turns out to be constructed by language that shapes our perception of the world. We tend to mistake our "inner reality" for what actually happens.

As I mentioned at the start of this chapter: Language, whether expressed through self-talk or conversation with others, shapes our destiny. Bringing awareness to what we say really matters, and allows us to gain quicker access to our psychic and intuitive abilities.

Reader Notes

Chapter 5

Mindfulness & Intuitive Heart

"Your vision will become clear
only when you can look into your own heart.
Who looks outside, dreams;
who looks inside, awakes."
~ Carl Jung

Nine-year-old Emerson left the Intuitive Development workshop excited and eager to demonstrate what he'd learned. He looked at me and smiled. "I'm going to do this when I'm scared." Emerson used the Mindfulness and Intuitive Heart exercises illustrated in this chapter to calm and relax his fears and anxiety.

Our young people, from a very early age, need to be empowered and taught self-awareness and responsibility. One day, while working with a group of kindergarteners, Rachel and John had an altercation and John came to me in tears.

"Rachel said I'm stupid and she doesn't want to be my friend." He could hardly speak through his tears.

I met his eyes. "Tell me what happened. I'm not going to be mad at you and you're not in trouble."

He looked at me in disbelief, "I'm *not* going to get in trouble?"

"No, you're not," I assured him. "Just tell me exactly what happened."

"I wanted to play with Rachel and Amy. They told me to go away. I got angry and knocked down their block building."

"Oh, you got angry because they didn't play with you," I rephrased.

"Yes," he said.

"What did you think when she called you stupid and told you to go away?" I asked.

"That she doesn't like me," he replied.

"Let's find out what Rachel thinks," I told him. I called Rachel over. "Rachel, I'm going to ask you a few questions. You're not in trouble and there is nothing wrong. Is John your friend?"

She smiled. "Yes."

"Do you like playing with him?"

"Yes."

"Did you call him stupid and tell him to go away?"

She shuffled a bit and looked down. "Amy and I wanted to play by ourselves today. We told him we wanted to play together without anyone else today. He got angry and knocked over the blocks. I called him stupid and told him to go away."

I looked at John. "Rachel likes you, did you hear that? Did she tell you she wanted to play with Amy by herself?"

"Yes."

"Do you think it's okay, to just play with one friend sometimes?"

"Yes," he said. His next statement displayed real emotional intelligence. "I'm sorry, Rachel. My feelings were hurt 'cause I thought you didn't want to be my friend."

"I'm your friend, John. I just wanted to play with Amy today."

"I'm sorry I knocked over your blocks."

"I'm sorry I called you stupid."

That was it. This conversation took about five minutes. They left happily and resumed playing, all doing their own thing.

Every day, we make things mean something. Someone once said: "Humans are meaning-making creatures." I agree. We attach meaning to almost everything, imposing patterns and meaning everywhere because we long to make sense of our world. But we often forget that the meaning we impose expresses *our* point of view.

John and Rachel's conversation went smoothly because they had been practicing Mindfulness and Intuitive Heart Training. They were taught to assume personal responsibility for their thoughts and actions.

Mindfulness practice can teach children to achieve a level of self-awareness and self-responsibility. In the Intuitive Heart Practice, we learn to listen to important messages from the heart. We learn compassion and connection.

Mindfulness is not meditation. It is a method of quieting the mind and bringing awareness to our thoughts, feelings, and inner world—an effective way to bring awareness to one's self. Mindfulness teaches us to become present, and to connect with our higher Self. During mindfulness, we can focus our awareness either on an inner sound, such as our breathing, on an outside sound (for example, airplanes, the wind, birds, people in another room) or whatever we choose to focus on.

Mindfulness affects our body chemistry and physiology in such a way that it tends to create a sense of peace. When I practice mindfulness with children, I have them focus on various scenes, sounds, breathing, feelings, and thoughts, as I teach them to relax both their bodies and their minds. This truly marks the beginning of their journey inward. They learn focus, concentration, self-awareness, and the art of *being*.

We live in a world ruled by doing and action. In mindfulness practice, I teach children to become the observers of behavior and situations, rather than *being* those behaviors. For example, when we think of ourselves as "hurt" or "angry," we believe those emotions are real. When we enter into a mindfulness practice, we experience observing these emotions and can detach from them. We can witness ourselves not "being" those things, but rather the *witness* who experiences those emotions. We learn to disentangle ourselves from our stories of who we are and our views of the world. We learn to take responsibility, to become conscious, and to see the interconnectedness of all things.

My favorite mindfulness exercise begins by focusing on breathing. Mindfulness brings our awareness to the here and now. In the present moment, emotions—such as anger, upset, fear, etc.—do not have time to form. We simply *experience* whatever happens, such as our breathing.

At the end of this chapter, you will find scripts for Mindfulness and Intuitive Heart meditations that you can do with your child.

The Intuitive Heart Exercise teaches us to follow the flow of energy and breath. We learn to be still. We quiet our minds and learn to listen for messages from our heart. The Heart Math organization regularly conducts extensive research into the intelligence of the heart, intuition, and energetic connections. When using the Intuitive Heart Exercise, we recognize our heart as an important information organ. We receive knowledge through the heart as well as the brain. Have you ever heard someone say, "My heart wants me to…"?

With the Intuitive Heart Exercise, we practice listening for information delivered from the heart. We practice making a heart connection with ourselves, our intuition, other people, and situations.

In my workshops, children use mindfulness and intuitive heart to focus and project their thoughts and feelings to different parts of the planet. During the mindfulness, intuitive heart exercise, I've had children perform psychic healing on themselves, and remote healing for others and the planet (this was the case during the aftermath of a serious earthquake that frightened and upset the children). The exercise gave them peace of mind and directed their attention to contribute to healing and helping others.

I once worked with a group of twenty-two six-year-old children, one had Asperger's and another had autism. Their classroom teacher informed me that ever since she had started using this work with students, both children participated fully during the exercises. All the children reported feeling the presence of pure love and light energy.

One little girl, Eloise, expressed feeling and hearing her heart say, "Relax." Ryan said, "I felt love in my heart."

During one of our sessions, I introduced the children to the voices in their heads. Placing a sock puppet on my right hand, I began demonstrating some of the things we hear in our heads. I used a personal memory about the time I didn't want to publish my children's book, *Annabelle and the Domino*, because I feared children wouldn't like it. I pretended the sock spoke: "It's a silly book. No one is going to like it. You don't know how to write. No one will read your book."

The children burst out laughing and everyone wanted to share an experience.

Eliza shared how she had forgotten to brush her hair that morning and was sure everyone would laugh at her. Julie Ann said she heard her mother's voice in her head telling her, "Don't do that," and then she felt sad and bad.

I showed how these thoughts could go away and how we could change them to more empowering thoughts through mindfulness. We released the emotional charges and meanings from the experiences. Everyone present experienced a powerful and profound moment,

Mindfulness and Intuitive Heart open doorways that help us to develop intuition and other psychic abilities. The mind needs to be quieted and the heart needs to be opened in order for us to hear, process, and interpret the messages we receive from our human "satellite dish." Through Mindfulness and Intuitive Heart, children easily focus their attention and intention elsewhere and "project" it to specific parts of the planet.

Mindfulness brings huge benefits. Children learn to focus on being present in the moment. They learn to clear their minds of distractions and worries. This allows them to be more present when they work on tasks, and it brings another dimension to learning. Incorporating mindfulness in the classroom has very real physical benefits, too. Scientists have learned that a consistent mindfulness routine affects areas in the brain associated with learning, memory, and emotions, as well as the functioning of the immune system.

Every teacher knows all-too-well the problems that plague our educational system. Children suffer because of the pressure placed on testing. Both educators and parents condition our children to believe that power and success in life can be achieved only by getting higher test scores. Nothing could be farther from the truth.

We can, and need to, change these educational requirements through increased awareness. Learning how to tap into psychic and intuitive abilities, inherent in each of us, will change the current educational paradigm. It is only a matter of time and awareness.

The following suggestions will help as you practice Mindfulness and Intuitive Heart exercises regularly throughout your day. And remember: a simple and short mindfulness routine can bring significant benefits both mentally and physiologically.

- Begin with a simple yoga pose or sit with your back straight (in a chair with your feet touching the ground).
- Practice learning to run energy through your body (see Chapter 6). Practice the Simple "Intuitive Heart" exercise (see Chapter 6).
- Do a quick Mindfulness and Intuitive Heart exercise (five to seven minutes) prior to school (or work) in the morning, then after school, and before starting homework activities, and also before going to bed.

Use Intuitive Heart throughout the day. You will find this especially powerful when feeling disempowered (see Chapter 6).

And now it's time to practice.

Reader Notes

_____
_____
_____
_____
_____
_____
_____
_____
_____
_____
_____
_____
_____
_____
_____
_____
_____
_____
_____
_____
_____
_____
_____

Chapter 6

Getting into Action
(Fun Activities to Develop
and Enhance Intuition)

"In each of us are places where we have never gone.
Only by pressing the limits do you ever find them."
~ Dr. Joyce Brothers, American psychologist,
television personality, and columnist

Janine, a twelve-year-old participant in one of my workshops shared: "This was the best class I've ever had in all my life. I learned so much about what my mind can do. I'm going to remember this day forever!" I clearly intend that you and your children experience this, too. Below are some of the exercises I use in my workshops with children. They all begin with meditation, mindfulness, or intuitive heart exercises. To help you get started, I also include scripts for the mindfulness and intuitive heart exercises.

Exercise 1: Still and Quiet, Calm and Controlled
(ages three and up):

Objective: Children learn to control their bodies. Learning to control one's body takes practice and self-discipline; a key factor of emotional intelligence.

Activity: Children sit "crisscross applesauce," also known as "easy pose" (*sukhasana* in yoga). They place their fingers in the "zoot" position (tips of the first three fingers touching each other), resting their hands on their knees. I then have the children stare at an object without moving their bodies. Three-year-olds start for fifteen seconds without moving and gradually work up to one minute. For older children and adults, incorporating a candle helps focus attention. Candle-focus lowers brainwaves into the alpha state (see Chapter 2 on the brain). Next, I have children extend the time they sit by thirty seconds to a minute for each session, with the objective of focusing and controlling the body for at least ten minutes (no scratching, no wiggling). This takes practice, even for

dults. The longer you can sit still as an adult, the deeper
will go into trance.

You can also download apps for Candle Focus.

Exercise 2: Let's Communicate
(ages three and up):

Objective: Children learn to practice telepathic
communication. For psychic development and intuition,
we need to cultivate telepathy. In our groups, we practice
learning to receive and send messages between one another.

Cut out simple card squares in the following colors:
red, blue, black, green, yellow. Children receive one set
of cards (the receivers). You (as sender) will have another
matching set. In your mind's eye, chose one of the colors
and focus on silently saying and imaging the color. (For
this exercise, it helps when children cover their eyes with
simple blinders). Give them a minute or so and then have
them remove their blinders and tell you which color they
saw.

Switch roles. With practice, you will see improve-
ment. This develops the skill of clairvoyance and telepathic communication.

You can vary this activity, for example by "sending"
and "receiving" numbers and objects. When using an ob-

ject, have the children draw what they see, rather than label it.

With practice, you can then progress to sending and receiving scenes. Cut out pictures from a magazine and place them in an envelope. Children can then draw what they "see."

Exercise 3: Find the Hidden Object
(ages three and up):

Objective: Children will find a hidden object—a variation of the hot/cold game. The directions differ because the child will be guided to find the object through telepathic instructions rather than using sensory cues like saying "hot/getting hotter" or "cold/getting colder." In the early stages, limit the size of the area to avoid frustration and the risk of giving up.

With older children, you can turn this game into a variation of "Hide and Seek." Have the older children pretend practicing to connect with the energy of the hidden object.

Exercise 4: Simple Mindfulness

Script: We will now introduce a simple exercise for practicing mindfulness by learning to focus on sounds outside and inside you. First, let's get into our mindful

out through your nose and through your body and you
don't have to do a thing.

Your body possesses natural intelligence. It knows
just what to do and it knows just what it needs. Notice the
breath as it comes in and out. Feel how relaxed your body
becomes as you follow the flow of the air (inhalation).
Just relax and allow the breath to flow naturally through
your body. Your body breathes this way when you sleep.
Right now, you are awake as you watch the flow of the
air enter your body as you relax with each breath. Whenever you need to relax, you can silently say the word "relax" and your body will do so, just like now. You can
learn to trust your body knowing that the next breath will
come in automatically and will flow through your body
giving you life and energy. As you release the air, more
and more will come back on its own and you can let go
again. Air comes back as a gift. Life comes as a gift. As
you release the air, you make room for new air to come in
again. Imagine saying "thank you" to the air as it comes
into your body and "thank you" as it leaves. Visualize the
air flowing through your body and going to your heart.
Imagine the air circling your heart.

Now focus on the sounds you hear outside. What do you hear? [Allow your child to spend at least thirty seconds to a minute doing this.]

Now focus on the sounds you hear inside your body. Can you hear your breathing?

I will now count backwards from five to one. When I reach one, you will open your eyes, feeling wide awake, and better than before. Five, feeling good...four, feeling alert and wide awake...three...two...one. Eyes open, wide awake, feeling better than before.

Discussion: Encourage your child to share his/her experience. Remember, never try to correct someone's experience. It's just that: *their experience.* It's neither right nor wrong. It may not be your experience. Do not judge, criticize, or invalidate any of their experiences. The "gold," the value, comes from listening to your child share the experience and then acknowledging him or her by saying, "Thank you for sharing your experience."

Exercise 5: Body Mindfulness

Objective: To focus on bodily sensations.

Use the script from the "Simple Mindfulness" exercise above. Then ask the following while they sit relaxed:

"What do you feel in your body?" These will be physical feelings. Perhaps a leg hurts from sitting too long. Perhaps another physical sensation now enters their awareness. Are they hot, cold, just right?

Exercise 6: Intuitive Heart
(Created by Dr. Henry Reed)

Objective: To receive the message your heart sends.

Children sit in easy yoga pose. Fingers in the zoot position with the first three finger-tips touching; hands resting gently on the knees. I like to use quiet, meditative music in the background.

Script: Sit in the mindful body position. Fingers in the zoot position. Now close your eyes and feel the air enter through your nose. Notice how your breath naturally flows in and out through your nose and you don't have to do a thing. Notice how your breath naturally flows in and out, through your nose and through your body and you don't have to do a thing.

Let go of any control over your breathing and simply watch it happen by itself. Allow yourself to discover the natural flow of your breathing. Allow yourself to go with the flow. The breath naturally comes and goes, and the natural flow has a lot to teach you.

Let's begin by placing your focus on the exhalation, breathing out. Notice how the breath flows out, a natural letting go. A relaxation. Let the exhalation teach you how to relax, to let go. With each exhalation, you learn how to relax a little bit more. As the breath goes out and you re-lax, release all control over your breathing. You can now accept the incoming of the next breath.

Let each incoming breath arrive on its own, in its own time. Let each incoming breath teach you how to accept, how to receive.

As the breath goes out, relax and let go and wait for the next incoming breath to come on its own. Let go of any need to make the inhalation happen according to your will and simply accept the incoming breath as it comes on its own.

Each cycle of breathing gives you another opportuni-ty to experience the relaxation of letting go and trusting the next breath to come on its own. Discover for yourself that you can trust the next breath to come on its own.

Experience the next breath as taking care of itself, taking care of you, removing the old air and bringing in new air. Experience the breath as a gift, taking care of you, cleansing you, renewing you, and bringing the gift of life. Enjoy the breath of life. Enjoy the gift of life com-ing to you. Life breathes you.

Spirit breathes you. Experiment for a moment with the feeling of gratitude for this gift of life. Just allow yourself to feel grateful for the gift of life coming to you freely, giving you what you need.

See what it's like to experience gratitude for the breath that comes to you as a gift. Give yourself permission to enjoy the feeling of gratitude. Focus your feelings of gratitude in the area of your heart. Let your heart be the center of your experience of gratitude and notice how your heart responds. Allow gratitude to soften your heart. Allow your heart to become warm, expanding, blossoming with love. Allow your entire body to harmonize with this feeling of love.

With your heart now open, you become a channel of love. Discover the higher consciousness that lives in your open heart. Listen as your heart speaks to you. Feel the love flowing through your heart as it gives you an important message now.

Accept the truth of your heart. Accept this opportunity to allow the higher consciousness of love to bring you needed wisdom or inspiration. What message does your heart deliver to you? [Allow a few minutes here for them to receive a message.]

Thank your heart for this important message you have received today. You can even allow the corners of your lips to soften into a smile, while you think of the message your heart has sent you. [Allow time here before transitioning to the close.]

I will now count backwards from five to one. When I reach one, you will open your eyes, feeling wide awake, and better than before. Five, feeling good...four, feeling alert and wide awake...three...two...one. Eyes open, wide awake, feeling better than before.

Ask the children to share the messages they received.

Reader Notes

Chapter 7

Trusting Intuition
(Access and Develop Your Inner Power
for Future Success)

"If the doors of perception were cleansed,
everything would appear to man as it is: infinite."
~ William Blake

In 2003, Japanese scientists discovered pentaquarks, made up of four quarks and an antiquark, the smallest particles of matter. I believe there will always be smaller parts to discover as physicists continue to explore inside atoms. Scientists claim that the most powerful force in nature, the *strong nuclear force,* holds these pentaquarks together. In this chapter, we will explore a very different kind of force—something within us that shows up in lucid dreaming, out-of-body experiences (OBEs), telekinesis, seeing auras, and psychometry.

Each of us possesses a kind of "inner force"—essentially, what many people call "the power of the mind" or "mind over matter"—that when directed and focused can produce exceptional results. When called upon (for example in emergencies), it can empower us to lift cars, or endure to survive against all odds, or heal from incurable illnesses. We all can draw from a strength within, a possibly unlimited force we might not even imagine we possess. We can call on this force to will events, to heal others and ourselves, and to create miracles and magic.

We can also call on this force to create out-of-body experiences. An OBE can occur during some traumatic event (such as life-or-death surgery) or spontaneously for no particular reason. Usually, it comes with an experience of one's mind or consciousness being outside the body, watching from a distant vantage point. When this happens, we experience a sensation of floating and flying.

In order to achieve an OBE at will, you must practice: Prior to going to sleep, tell yourself you will have an out-of-body experience. You could use a well-known method developed by author and mystic Robert Bruce called the "rope technique." Picture a rope hanging from the ceiling. Now, while lying in bed and using your imaginary hands, visualize yourself climbing the rope, until you have left your body, and can see it beneath you. Although relaxed, do not fall asleep. See yourself traveling beyond your body. Make a note of what you see, hear, or smell. Enjoy the visualization.

You can also achieve an OBE through lucid dreaming—a dream in which you are aware you are dreaming. Have you ever had the experience of waking up at a point in your dream, knowing you are dreaming, and then re-entering the dream where you left off? Psychologists recognize this as a form of lucid dreaming. Alternatively, you can tell yourself you will have a highly specific dream, and then you do. Priming the mind like this can produce extraordinary results.

While viewing events and people within a lucid dream, you know your real body continues to lie in bed, relaxed. In many ways, it's similar to being in a virtual reality. To help you prepare for lucid dreaming, you can also use an audio recording specifically designed for getting into an alpha state, and then practice going deeper into theta (see Chapter 2 on how the brain works).

People often use lucid dreams to explore and resolve their own or others' problems. In some of my workshops, we practice dreaming for other participants. This form of lucid dreaming works effectively because we all connect through consciousness.

Now let's turn to psychometry. This refers to an ability to read the energy of a person or situation by holding or touching an object belonging to the person or entity in question. You can practice psychometry in a few ways. For example, ask someone to bring you a small object to practice on. Take the object, hold it in your hands, and allow any information and impressions to come to you. Do not judge yourself, second guess, or filter any of the information you receive. Merely report what you see, feel, sense, or hear, while holding the object. As with other forms of psi, this too, takes practice.

Telekinesis refers to the ability to move objects at a distance by mental power alone. I became fascinated with this after reading Robert Heinlein's *Stranger in a Strange Land.* I have personally witnessed telekinesis three times with children under the age of eight using a domino. This, too, takes practice. I recommend meditation as an effective way to prepare your mind for telekinesis. Once your mind is clear and settled, then visualize the outcome you want. Next, practice building energy between your hands. Rub your palms together until you can feel heat and energy coming off them. Now direct this energy toward an object you wish to move.

In workshops, I have the children practice this with standing dominos. This process can take up to twenty minutes or more merely directing the energy at the object.

As always, practice (coupled with clear intention) lays a strong foundation for success in telekinesis.

Finally, many people find it easier to see auras—best done from a quiet, comfortable position. Choose a suitable object to begin your aura practice. A great example to start with: Look at the top of a tree in the distance and allow your eyes to gently go out of focus. Within a few seconds, you will see a shadow a few inches above the tree (looks like its outline). That's its aura. With continued practice and time, you will begin to see auras around other objects and people. With more practice, the silver/gray shade will take on colors.

To practice on humans and pets: Choose a place around the head of the animal (best if your pet is sitting still or sleeping) and allow your eyes to go out of focus. Now see the silver/gray light around its form. You may begin to notice a change in the color variations around your pet. This same technique applies to humans, too. Try practicing this in a large waiting area with many people. They need never know you use the opportunity to test your ability to see their auras.

With practice and perseverance, you and your child will begin to develop, enhance, and use, your amazing psychic and intuitive abilities.

Reader Notes

BIBLIOGRAPHY

Alder, Vera Stanley. *From the Mundane to the Magnificent*. London: Rider, 1979.

Boroditsky, Lera. *How language shapes thought. Scientific American*, February, 2011.

Buchanan, Lyn. *The Seventh Sense: The Secrets of Remote Viewing*. New York: Pocket Books, 2003.

Choquette, Sonia. *The Answer is Simple. Love Yourself, Live Your Spirit*. New York: Hay House, 2008.

Choquette, Sonia. *Trust Your Vibes: Secret Tools for Sixth Sensory Living*. New York: Hay House, 2004.

Coyle, Daniel. *The Talent Code*. New York: Bantam Books, 2009

Dispenza, Joe, Dr. *Breaking the Habit of Being Yourself*. New York: Hay House Inc., 2012

Dispenza, Joe, Dr. *Evolving Your Brain*. Florida: Health Communications Inc., 2007

Dispenza, Joe, Dr. *You Are the Placebo*. New York: Hay House Inc., 2014

Fodor, Jerry. "The Language of Thought Hypothesis," Stanford Encyclopedia of Philosophy. Sep. 2010

Gardner, Howard. *Five Minds for the Future*. Cambridge: Harvard Business School, 2006.

Harris, Paul L. *Trusting What You're Told: How Children Learn from Others*. Cambridge: Belknap Press, 2012.

Hawkins, David R. *Power vs. Force*. Sedona: Veritas Publishing, 1987.

Hill, Napoleon. *Think and Grow Rich*. New York: Random House, 1960.

Hunt, Valerie. *Infinite Mind, The Science of Human Vibrations*. Malibu: Malibu Publishing, 1989.

Jung, Carl Gustav. *Man and His Symbols*. New York: Anchor Press 1964.

Levine, Melvin D. *A Mind at a Time*. New York: Simon & Schuster, 2002.

Lipton, Bruce. *The Biology of Belief.* Carlsbad: Hay House, 2008.

Maltz, Maxwell. *Psycho-Cybernetics.* New York: Simon & Schuster. 1960.

Misset, Bill. *Awakening the Soul. Book One.* Bloomington, IN.: AuthorHouse, 2008.

Mlodinow, Leonard. *The Drunkard's Walk. How Randomness Rules our Lives.* New York: Pantheon Books, 2008.

Mlodinow, Leonard. *Subliminal: How Your Unconscious Mind Rules Your Behavior.* New York: Random House, 2012.

Murphy, Joseph, Dr. T*he Power of Your Subconscious Mind.* New York: Bantam Books, 2001.

Nadeau, Robert & Kafatos, Menas. *The Non-Local Universe.* London: Oxford University Press, 1999.

Nilsson, Nils, J. *Understanding Beliefs.* Cambridge: MIT Press, 2014.

Pierce, Penny. *The Intuitive Way. The Definitive Way to Increasing Your Awareness*. New York: Atria Publishing/Beyond Words, 2009.

Pinker, Steven: *How the Mind Works*. New York: Norton, 2009.

Pinker, Steven: *Language Learnability*. Cambridge: Harvard University Press, 2009.

Pinker, Steven: T*he Language Instinct: How the Mind Creates Language*. New York: Harper Collins, 2010.

Reed, Henry. *The Intuitive Heart: How to Trust Your Heart for Guidance and Healing*. Virginia Beach: ARE Press, 2000.

Reed, Henry. *Channeling Your Higher Self* (Private Edition). Virginia Beach: ARE Press, 2007.

Robbins, Jim. *A Symphony in the Brain: The Evolution of the New Brainwave Biofeedback.* New York: Grove/Atlantic Press. 2014.

Schwartz, David. *The Magic of Thinking Big*. New York: Prentice Hall, 1959.

Swann, Ingo. *Everybody's Guide to Natural ESP*. New York: St. Martin's Press. 1991.

Targ, Russell and Puthoff, Harold E. *Mind Reach*. Berkeley: Hampton Roads Publishing, 2004.

Vygotsky, Lev. *Thought and Language*. Cambridge: MIT Press, 2012.

Weschcke, Carl Llewellyn and Slate, Joe E. *Psychic Empowerment for Everyone*. MN.: Llewellyn Publishers, 2009.

Wiseman, Sara. *Your Psychic Child*. Woodbury, MN: Llewellyn Publishers, 2010.

Wiseman, Sara. *Becoming Your Best Self. The Guide to Clarity, Inspiration and Joy*. Woodbury, MN: Llewellyn Publishers, 2012.

Yogananda, Paramahansa, Yogi. *Autobiography of a Yogi*. CA.: Self Realization Fellowship, 1974.

About the Author

For thirty-seven years, pioneering teacher, intuitive advisor, psychic, and author Elly Molina has worked with children to develop their powerful intuitive abilities. She consistently integrates Mindfulness and Intuitive Heart exercises into her educational practice. A staunch advocate of everyone using intuition and natural psychic capacities, Molina empowers children and adults whenever she can—for example, in workshops and classes, speaking engagements, as well as through private consultations. Molina has appeared on ABC, NBC, CBS, FOX, and in the *New York Times*. In 2015, the International Remote Viewing Association (IRVA) Conference in New Orleans featured her as a speaker/presenter.

Made in the USA
San Bernardino, CA
21 March 2017